Tara Becker's mission to empower and inspire women is beautifully woven through her new book *The Journey from Fear to Freedom*. Through her own search for the authentic life she has create a delightful map for other women to follow.

Zoilita Grant,
Speaker/Coach
www.zoilitagrant.net

It is with profound elation and gratitude that I am asked to comment on this book. I am gratified to know that Tara's dedication to her dream has given her the strength and fortitude to undertake this journey to self awareness and growth. I applaud all that she has written from her heart and deepest conviction. She is shining the light for all of us to follow her story and to emulate her understanding of what it takes to find the truth and meaning in life. I am proud of her journey and hope those who seek their path will find gems of wisdom and sacrifice in this book. Good on you Tara ---you go girl.

Dr. Anastasia Alexander

In the great scheme of "don't take yourself too damn seriously", Tara Becker's wit and wisdom are a joy. As each life is fraught with its own trials and tribulations Tara refrains from singling out her own challenges as exceptional, rather they are the guideposts and the vehicles she employs on her journey of self-awareness. You will find yourself in her story and recognize some common road signs on the journey. Enjoy.

Ken Ludwig
- Inspiring speaker, Health & Fitness Coach,
Co-Founder of Vibrant Aging
teamrockitnow@gmail.com

This book is a fun, authentic look at how Tara turned her life into a place of joy, passion and ultimate freedom. Tara provides you with easy to follow, empowering tools that will help any woman step into the life they desire and deserve. It's time to claim your freedom!

Karen Rudat,
Empowerment Coach
www.karenrudat.com

The book, The Journey from Fear to Freedom is a refreshing reminder of how powerful we are when we connect from within and stop living out of fear. When that connection is lost it affects every area of our lives. Tara addresses each of these with powerful easy to implement tools to assist us on this journey. Take advantage of this book, study it, complete the exercises within it and you'll be sure to soar right into the Freedom you have longed for and deserve.

Kristina Darling,
Entrepreneur, Speaker & Coach
www.kristinadarling.com

"Fear to Freedom" is an inspirational book about how to stay connected to your truth, your dreams, and your freedom. Tara shares the importance of remembering who you are, and how to move through your fears into a life of empowerment. Instead of living life by default, she shows you how to move forward by consciously choosing new perspectives, new beliefs, and new behaviors to support you in your personal and professional success. Her book reminds us that living life to the fullest is an option and you get to choose.

Barbara Daoust,
Author, Speaker, & Success Coach
www.barbaradaoust-tir.com

Jump in and enjoy Tara Becker's guidance as she shares wise words and personal experiences of moving from fear to freedom. Creatively designed, you will enjoy the lessons and suggestions she has created. A well-written, heartfelt book to inspire you to go for what you really want in life.

Lisa J. Shultz,
Author and Speaker
www.lisajshultz.com

The journey of being a woman is complex, to say the least; however, the journey from fear to freedom is, well, a story all unto itself. Tara beautifully shares her personal journey of fear that caused her to lose herself, deal with the loss of her love, as well as losing everything in between. Within each chapter, however, Tara's wisdom, wit, straight forward no-nonsense sense of humor, and love to inspire and heal comes shining through. Whatever journey you are on now, as you read through Tara's journey, you will feel a deep connection to her because she understands. In Tara's understanding, you'll find support, encouragement, and the courage to move to your next level of life... Freedom!

Dr. Anita M. Jackson,
Founder, Your Feminine Success
Empire Building Coach
www.dranitamjackson.com

TARA BECKER

THE JOURNEY
from *Fear*
to
Freedom

A Woman's Guide to Rediscovering
the Life She Always Imagined

BALBOA.
PRESS
A DIVISION OF HAY HOUSE

Balboa Press books may be ordered through booksellers or by contacting:

Balboa Press
A Division of Hay House
1663 Liberty Drive
Bloomington, IN 47403
www.balboapress.com
1 (877) 407-4847

Because of the dynamic nature of the Internet, any web addresses or links contained in this book may have changed since publication and may no longer be valid. The views expressed in this work are solely those of the author and do not necessarily reflect the views of the publisher, and the publisher hereby disclaims any responsibility for them.

The author of this book does not dispense medical advice or prescribe the use of any technique as a form of treatment for physical, emotional, or medical problems without the advice of a physician, either directly or indirectly. The intent of the author is only to offer information of a general nature to help you in your quest for emotional and spiritual well-being. In the event you use any of the information in this book for yourself, which is your constitutional right, the author and the publisher assume no responsibility for your actions.

Any people depicted in stock imagery provided by Getty Images are models, and such images are being used for illustrative purposes only. Certain stock imagery © Getty Images.

This book is a work of non-fiction. Unless otherwise noted, the author and the publisher make no explicit guarantees as to the accuracy of the information contained in this book and in some cases, names of people and places have been altered to protect their privacy.

Print information available on the last page.

ISBN: 978-1-5043-9962-3 (sc)
ISBN: 978-1-5043-9961-6 (hc)
ISBN: 978-1-5043-9960-9 (e)

Library of Congress Control Number: 2018904613

Balboa Press rev. date: 07/24/2018

Contents

For all of my sisters
around the world.

Foreword

After years of seeking the answers to her internal struggles, Tara stepped onto the path of inner awareness, self-realization, and action. She had always put the needs of others ahead of her own, thereby hindering her ability to find the joy in living. She has discovered that freedom comes from a place inside and that each one of us already has a full-access pass!

Tara has taken the time and energy to read, listen, attend workshops, watch videos, and participate in the trainings of some of the best experts in the field of personal growth, spiritual advancement, and relationship mastery.

Tara shares with you stories of her life, allowing you to understand how she can show you the way from Fear to Freedom! She is familiar with many of the experiences that you may be living through now: heartache and heartbreak, betrayal, not feeling heard, anxiety, unable to speak your truth, the loss of a loved one, and financial hardship. Tara uses what she has learned to guide you along on your journey of living in happiness and contentment.

Tara has committed to putting her energetic support behind you every step of the way. She will touch your heart and soul as she connects with you through words and videos. You can feel it!

In this book, Tara honors the people from whom she learned this wisdom and gives you their names so that, if you wish to delve deeper, you have what you need. She is your cosmic reporter on this planet that we call life!

Her practical advice enables you to move toward freedom in every moment! When you are in action, fear falls away. She also shares little-known and easy-to-follow secrets of manifesting the life of your dreams.

I am grateful to have been, at different times, a teacher, a trainer, a coach, a friend, and a soul sister of Tara's. I am privileged to also be her student and learn from the lessons that she shares with the world in this book.

The winds of change are upon us. Tara is an expert at having fun, riding the waves, and keeping her head up so that she can see the light and the sun. Let her take you for an extraordinary Journey from Fear to Freedom!

Jade Rehder, CCC, CT, MAT
5D Consciousness Coach, Trainer, and
Advance Hawaiian Huna Practitioner
www.JadeRehder.com

CHAPTER ONE

From Fear to Faith

Not long ago, I stood exactly where you may be now. I was living a life of suffering and loneliness. I had done all the right things, read all the right books, gone to all the right workshops, and watched all the right movies, but I was still miserable. It felt as if I waited for my authentic life to start, like I lamented on the sidelines with no idea how to get into the game.

I was always busy, weighed down by the daily tasks of being a mom, a wife, and a businesswoman, yet I never seemed any closer to fulfilling any of my true desires. I was plagued by feeling like a failure and feeling inadequate and stupid. No matter how good I was at something, I beat myself up for not being better. I suffered from a crippling case of perfectionism.

My fears overwhelmed me every day: fear of success, fear of being abandoned, fear of being laughed at, fear of not living up to others' expectations, fear of losing the man I loved, fear of being left alone, fear of being humiliated. Let's face it, I was afraid of being alive!

How had I gotten to such a place? How had I become a woman frightened of everything? Where was that radiant, confident woman I knew I was supposed to grow up to be? I had gotten seriously off course! I had to find my way back to the real me.

Like most women, I knew I was meant for bigger things. I had always searched for that higher calling, and I knew other women searched for it, also. I wanted to let go of my ego and find myself again. I wanted to get out of my own way and be that person who lived in fun, joy, abundance, light, and love.

I've been holding my emotions within myself since I was five years old. I remember a time when I knew it was not okay to show my emotions. My parents had hired a babysitter for me so they could go out on a date. I was ticked off they would leave me with someone I barely knew and were going out without me. I went into my bedroom and threw a royal temper-tantrum, hurling my stuffed animals all over my room. When my dad came in to say goodbye, he asked me what I was doing.

I lied to him about my feelings of sadness and anger. "Oh, I'm just playing a game."

When I was a senior in high school, I remember making a conscious decision not to dream anymore because many times in the past I had dreams, and they had never come true. Why continue to dream when I would always be disappointed?

Since that time years ago, I was already stifling my emotions and not dreaming; I was miles away from the person I wanted to be. I had to break through all that and learn to be myself. I had to do it not just for myself, but for women everywhere who have lost their way and have given to everyone and everything except themselves.

This book relates my quest into my authenticity, my fun, my power, my love, and my bliss. I invite you to go along on this odyssey with me.

Spirit is connected to everything.

Spirit being connected to everything was a new way of thinking for me. That said, I believe "we are spiritual beings having a human experience," which I didn't entirely understand until March 2008. That phrase was on a bumper sticker on my son's girlfriend's car.

Like most Judeo-Christians I had grown up with, and for most my adult life, I believed God was an entity people prayed to, and if they were good enough, did good works, and behaved correctly, God would answer their prayers.

In reality, the subconscious is an emotionless database of stored programs, whose function is strictly concerned with reading environmental signals and engaging in hardwired behavioral programs, no questions asked, no judgments made. The subconscious mind is a programmable 'hard drive' into which our life experiences are downloaded.
~ Bruce Lipton, *The Biology of Belief*

God was outside me, my judge and jury. Now I believe God is everything. We live out our lives as human avatars to encounter that which spirit cannot. As in the movie *City of Angels*, as spiritual beings, we do not feel emotions, such as love, happiness, anger, or sadness. As humans, we feel emotions, and we cannot appreciate one emotion without feeling its opposite, yin and yang.

There is one universal subconscious mind, and it is not personal.

Letting go is difficult. I should know. I've been attempting it for months. Letting go takes a shitload of courage that, oftentimes, I feel I do not possess. Somehow, I have always known the answers are inside me. I have determined all I need to do is give myself permission! I know this may sound suspiciously like psycho-babble and perhaps a bit too easy. It's okay to let go of the old patterns and messages that have guided you your entire life.

Take the leap! If you're anything like me, and I speculate you are, change things up! I couldn't continue any longer on the same approach. I couldn't take it anymore. I had to let go in order to take the next step and make for myself the life I had always imagined. It took practice.

I make it happen.

My mantra is *Practice Makes Permanent.* Making a change will feel strange for a while. Little by little, it will get easier. I will warn you, when you come to a fork in the road with a big lesson to be learned, it will feel really crappy. I've noticed lately when I'm working through a monster lesson, it rears its ugly head again, and again, and again. This would be the time to recall the movie *Groundhog Day* with Bill Murray. Heck, I've had the same lesson crash my party unannounced three times within forty-eight hours! And then, I get it. I need to learn this lesson now. I constantly remind myself there's no going back to my old way of doing things.

I never know when I will *get it* and will have finally learned any given lesson, thus seeming to make life a bit smoother. I am sure, to some degree, it may *appear* to be making life smoother. It's really that I aspire to travel through these lessons with grace and detachment and be grateful for the teaching. The burden of the lessons then feels less onerous.

Through studying under Master Zhi Gang Sha, it has become apparent to me as a spiritual being, who has been awakened to this adventure, I will struggle with enormous lessons with more difficulty and with greater frequency. However, I know the time will come when the ebb and flow of life's challenges will become more manageable. I am confident I will, at some point, reach that stage in my life. It may not happen in a year from now, but what if it happens at 3:00 this afternoon? Wouldn't that be amazing!

Dr. Wayne Dyer, *Change Your Thoughts, Change Your Life*
https://www.youtube.com/watch?v=tRRKonleAjA

By reading and listening to books by Dr. Wayne Dyer, I have learned, life's about changing how I see myself so all my dreams will become reality. This is in direct opposition to what my ego wants.

The closer I get to who I am, the more my ego shows itself. Pretend my thoughts and dreams are the software and whatever I want to program my life to be will become reality. First, I have to truly believe it with every fiber of my being. I do a silent meditation, which helps me to create my new reality. I will explain at the end of this chapter.

I wrote this book hoping to give you the guts to take the journey from fear to freedom. Is it worth it? Ummmm, let me think about that for a second. Yes, it's worth it!

Every life happening is a gift.
It may show up wrapped
in porcupine paper with thorn-covered ribbon.
Every gift is a treasure.
It is important to concentrate on the gift
and not on the wrapping.

Don't wait until circumstances are perfect to begin living your life. They never will be. My husband was diagnosed with cancer in March 2011. I became his primary caretaker and nursed him until he passed away on January 2, 2012. A year of doubt, pain, grief, and sorrow followed. I felt like I would never see the beauty in a sunset or feel a smile spread across my face again.

When someone close to you dies, it is natural to think about your own life. In my marriage, I was always waiting for the other shoe to drop. Waiting for the disaster that had to be just around the corner. I always thought another woman would take him from me. It never dawned on me it would be cancer.

My marriage was far from ideal. Hell, I couldn't even spell ideal at the time. Rick, my husband, had many great qualities, and I loved him dearly, but he was never faithful to me. He was never the husband I wanted him to be. And, he never made amends for his infidelities over the years. After spending sixteen years together, I felt helpless.

And yet, through the depths of my misery, I heard a quiet voice in my head, a voice I had not heard since I was a child. It told me I was about to change, that in the midst of all of the suffering, I could find the opportunity not just to survive but to thrive! For the first time in years, I decided to listen to that voice in my head.

Then, one morning soon after his passing, I awoke to a profound thought. It was awful. I could not deny it was true. Rick had made the ultimate sacrifice so I could discover the person I was meant to be. I know this sounds strange and perhaps harsh. However, I wouldn't share it with you if I didn't believe it from the bottom of my heart to be correct.

The world is full of miracles. Sometimes in order to see them, we need to look at the world differently. With my husband gone, I had no choice but to face my life, my genuine self. If Rick had not passed away, I would never have left him. I would never have embarked upon this venture. I would never have taken the spiritual route I have traversed these past years. I would never have learned such essential lessons, and you would not be reading this book.

The last two years have been an arduous, challenging time of self-exploration for me. I have spent a year and then some re-learning who I am, what I like, how I want to live, and what I want to be known for. I am finally becoming the person I was meant to be so I can do the work I was destined to perform! Thank you, Rick. I love you dearly. I miss you.

Courage Comes From Pain
~ Written inside a fortune cookie I got in November of 2012 while having lunch in Colorado with my close girlfriend, Kristina

I was ready to take the leap of faith. I had no choice. So, I jumped. Was I afraid? Are you kidding me? I was terrified! There are no words in Webster's Dictionary to describe the level of panic I was in. Dante himself could have constructed another circle in Hell just for me. The Universe had set me up perfectly for success. Without an escape hatch, without an armload of excuses, without a way to wiggle my way out of an uncomfortable situation, I was forced to take that surge and grow. I had a responsibility to become my best self, a responsibility we all share.

Katy Perry inspires us with *Firework*
https://youtu.be/QGJuMBdaqlw

I needed to be bold for only twenty seconds. I needed to corral the bravery to start. The Law of Attraction says: *That which is like unto itself is drawn. Whatever one gives their attention actualizes the experience.* Therefore, there is nothing you cannot be, do, or have. This is the Law of Attraction. I believe this, and it has become my guiding force in my life.

My inspiration comes from a song by Jana Stanfield, *Bring It On.* The lines from the song say, *I'm through grieving, I'm through dreaming that the life I had is ever coming back. No more wishin' on someone else's star that'll never be mine. I think it's time, so bring it on.* Nothing happens in life unless we first dream. Give this song a listen while you read the rest of this chapter. It will knock your spiffy striped socks right off.

Jana Stanfield, *Bring It On*
http://www.youtube.com/watch?v=XddvhDQI1oM

S.O.A.R.
Simply Open And Receive

After Rick's passing, it occurred to me, if I did not galvanize myself into action and start putting myself first, I could leave this life with my song unsung. I could die without having fulfilled my purpose and my passion. With my fingers bleeding as I clung to my past, I gasped... and then I finally let go.

Dr. Wayne Dyer, *How God tells you it's time for a change*
http://www.youtube.com/watch?v=J3bM8I7GzYM

I decided to redesign my life. I did just that and identified my official, bonafide self when writing this book. And, you know what? It was much more incredible than I ever thought it would be!

> *It is in the midst of transformation,*
> *the test is the most unpleasant.*

Every obstacle I thought stood in my way was actually a teacher, a guide, helping me build the life I wanted. I finally figured out all that anxiety and doubt was an illusion. Every second of every day, the Universe conspired with me to achieve success. All I needed to do was dismiss the doubting parts of myself that prevented me from seeing my genuine self. I had to get out of my own way and reject all those old messages that resided in my head that had been established by society, my family, and no longer served me and hadn't for quite some time.

I wanted to shout from the rooftops the only thing standing in the way of the life I truly desired was me. I needed to let go of the trepidation and step into freedom.

Most things in life don't turn out as we expect them to. Sometimes what happens instead is the good stuff. And, I'm convinced it's all good stuff.

> *We all deserve everything we've ever wanted!*

Please join me on a voyage of exploration in which I will walk you through the exact steps I took to give birth to the life I have always wanted. These steps are not theory or my version of armchair coaching. They are steps I actually took, steps that worked and continue to free me. They put me on the passage to living a life of bliss, abundance, love, and freedom I never thought possible. If these steps worked for me, they can work for you, too.

Someone once told me I was like a modern-day Joan of Arc. And, of course, I took that as a nice compliment. Honestly, I didn't know much about Joan of Arc, other than she had a passion for her purpose. She knew, no matter what she needed to fulfill her mission, she would gather people together to help her fulfill that mission.

I felt the Dalai Lama's statement, *the world will be saved by the western women*, was a call to action for me personally. That's why I am on this path right now, to share my story, teach others about what I have worked through and will continue to work through, and impart nuggets of wisdom about how my life is unfolding into the glorious life I was meant to live.

Decide who you want to be
and embrace the real you.

Here I am talking about how I am doing this for all women
all over the world. I am with you and here for you. I
continue to support you and am cheering you on.
www.tarabecker.com

Yes, it's work, and it is so worth it! I can't ever go back to the way things were before.

I put one foot in front of the other, and at times, the second foot is only inches behind the first. I do stumble and fall flat on my face. I pick myself up and do it all over again. I am a determined spitfire!

No matter what, I show up. I may not always have it all together, dressed to the nines with perfect hair and make-up, but I will always show up! I know you can, too.

I will be by your side and hold you up, so feel free to lean on me. I will always be in your corner cheering you on. You are me. I am you. We are one. My strength is your strength, and we are much stronger when we stand together. You can do it! I know I can, because I no longer have a choice. Are you ready to jump into freedom?

Letting Go = Freedom

Your soul wants you to know who you are. Peel away everything that isn't truly you to let your essence shine. Different elements comprise your identity, like the rainbow emanates from a crystal shining in the sun. Yet beneath it all is your spiritual core. Find your core, live life from your center. Don't try to expand your personal effectiveness and intent without first exploring and understanding the wisdom of your soul.

In my essence I am joy!

Following each chapter, I have provided you with exercises to help you begin your course to re-discovery. From my own efforts with letting go and lightening up, I know, if I give you a lengthy worksheet with lots of exercises on it, you won't do them. It's not you don't have the time. It's because, like me, the idea of letting go to really live scares the pants off you.

Kelly Clarkson singing *Stronger*
http://www.youtube.com/watch?v=Xn676-fLq7I

We'll take it nice and easy, keep it simple. You will need materials for these assignments, and we'll go over what they are in the instructions for each exercise. Let's get started!

Worksheets for Chapter One
Worksheet A: Your 22-Day Meditation Challenge

The 22-Day Meditation ~ Meditation is about quieting the mind and creating space in it for solitary thoughts. By stopping the *monkey mind* of craziness and endless negative ruminating, you open up room for new thoughts or ideas to come in. They say it takes 21 days to forge a new habit. I was challenged to a 22-day meditation disguised as a 21-day meditation. I'm doing the same for you.

Your meditation can be whatever you want it to be. I'll make a few suggestions but do what works for you. You could start with being quiet in a special place. It is not necessary to allow a large block of time. If you're new to meditating, you may wish to begin with a couple minutes then work your way up to more. I do recommend you get to the point where your meditation lasts at least ten minutes a day.

You could also draw an angel or tarot card and meditate on it. I did the 21-Day Meditation Challenge with Oprah Winfrey and Deepak Chopra. Please visit www.chopra.com and look for meditation challenges. These are wonderful guided meditations, and there are other great guided meditations elsewhere.

Worksheet B: The I AM Statements

I Am. This is what Dr. Wayne Dyer taught. If you can change your thoughts, you can change your life. As we learn in meditation, when we generate space in our minds, we need to put something back in. You don't want to leave a black hole where your thoughts were. We tend to make things up that aren't fact to clutter up our minds. Women especially do this. Replace those thoughts with new thoughts of you. Start by writing I Am statements. Mine look like this:

> *I Am Love.*
> *I Am Abundance.*
> *I Am Bliss.*
> *I Am Happiness.*
> *I Am Perfect Health.*
> *I Am Prosperity.*

Write everything in present tense. Go nuts. List as many as you can today. Then tomorrow, begin again. Write. Rinse. Repeat. I keep a journal, and each day I write as many I Am statements as I can until my hand cramps up where I can't possibility write one more word. If you find the going a bit slow in the beginning, try writing for two minutes. Then add a minute or two each time you write until you've built up to ten minutes consistently.

Dr. Wayne Dyer talks about the *I AM* exercise
https://www.youtube.com/watch?v=Y1RI2Q3KgWk

I Am Fun.
I Am Compassion.
I Am Confidence.
I Am Generosity.
I Am Enthusiasm.
I Am Worthy.
I Am Love.
I Am Enough.
I Am...
I Am...
I AM!

CHAPTER TWO

From Fear to Fun

I was raised believing you had to earn happiness. That is B.S.! I don't believe we came into these human bodies to be miserable.

Dance like there's nobody watching.
Love like you'll never get hurt.
Sing like there's nobody listening.
Live like it's Heaven on Earth.

Dr. Robert Holden, a world-renowned psychologist known for his work regarding happiness, once conducted an experiment on his patients. He asked those of his patients participating to allot one hour of their day to fun. That was all they had to do, nothing else, just have fun. The following week he checked in with his patients to see who had completed the task. Not a single patient had done the assignment! When he asked them why, they had the usual excuses: I didn't have enough time, I was too busy, I forgot.

He tried again. This time his patients only had to have fun for ten minutes a day. The next week he checked in once more.

Sheepishly, each patient reported he or she had not done the exercise. Not a single patient had found the time to have fun for just ten minutes a day.

Dr. Holden tried a third time. This time he told those patients they only had to have fun for one minute a day. Sixty seconds! Who couldn't find time for that?

Pleased with himself, Dr. Holden checked in with his patients the following week. He was sure they would all tell awesome stories about how they had completed the exercise and the delight they had felt in giving themselves this one small gift of a sixty-second fun break.

By the end of the day, Dr. Holden could hardly believe his ears. Once again, not a single patient had completed the exercise. Sixty seconds! They did not believe they deserved it. As their stories were told, Dr. Holden identified that his patients believed that fun and happiness had to be earned. Fun was a reward for working hard or suffering. You couldn't just have fun. That wasn't allowed. What a crock!

Where did this idea come from? Who was the numbskull who thought this up? The source of all of our anxieties stem from one single erroneous belief, that fun is earned. Don't you believe it! You deserve to have fun in every part of your life, right here, right now.

Listed here are the most common excuses for not having fun:

I don't deserve it.
I have to suffer first, then I can have fun.
There is too much suffering in the world for me to have a good time.
I can only have fun after I am perfect.
I can only have fun when my life is perfect.
I will have fun when I'm rich.
I can have fun only when I have no more problems.
I will have fun once I know I can never be hurt.

To have fun mocks others who are in anguish.

I bet you have used these excuses more than once. I know I use them all the time. Of course, I know now these excuses are laughable!

> *Yesterday is history.*
> *Tomorrow is a mystery.*
> *And today? Today is a gift.*
> *That's why they call it the present.*
> ~Babatunde Oatunji

Every moment you are not in the present and not sharing the gift of your happiness and presence is a moment wasted. The world is full of misery and lost souls. By choosing to be present and to live in the blessedness of the moment, you give others permission to do the same.

Babies show you how to do it right!
http://www.youtube.com/watch?v=uiws904iuEQ

The idea of having fun with everything I do came to me after reading *The Passion Test* by Chris and Janet Attwood. In accordance with the instructions in the book, I pinpointed what was most important in my life and boiled it down to five items, Chris and Janet call *passions*. They may also be known by other names, such as goals, dreams, intentions, wishes, or whatever name you would like to give them.

My first passion was to have fun with everything I do. Whenever I am faced with a decision, following Chris and Janet's lead, I opt in favor of my passion. I ask myself, *Will this be fun?* Having fun is one of my top five passions. If it isn't fun, why do it? When I decided to take this junket, I put having fun at the center of my life. Who says personal and spiritual growth has to be sad and somber? Lighten up!

Meet Janet Bray Attwood, co-author of *The Passion Test*
http://www.youtube.com/watch?v=qESq7Ob-whk

Not having fun with everything I do is like working at a job I don't like. I equate it to working Monday through Friday and living only for the weekend. Friday night is my big *woo-hoo*, but by the time Sunday morning rolls around, I'm all worked up about having to go to work the following day. I do not enjoy the second day of my weekend. I feel tightness in my chest and an ever-present cannonball in the pit of my stomach that frequently makes me want to blow chunks. That is, if I can even eat at all. A life like that is not worth living. You've got to have fun now!

Right now, exactly as you are, you deserve fun in your life. In fact, it is not only your right, it is your duty to find and follow your bliss. The world needs it, and the world needs you. Want to improve your life? Go have fun. Want to have more money? Go have fun. Want a better sex life, more free time, better inspiration? Want to save the world? Have fun!

Finding the fun and the merriment in your life right now gives you access to all of the information you seek. It removes negative energy, releases endorphins, lowers blood pressure, makes you look sexier (no, really, it does!), and frees you up to the boundless - intuitions that contain the solutions you and the world have been waiting for. Take a look at this video and get happy already!

Andy Dooley gets happy!
https://www.youtube.com/watch?v=P8ELFrExPng

Fun Is a Choice

Circumstances are never perfect. Our daily lives are plagued by constant failure. We never have enough money, time, or love. If you wait for the ideal conditions to be happy, you are in for a long haul, and I bet you have been waiting for a long, long time already. Everything is perfect for you at this time. You can't get more perfect than perfect, so choose fun!

How do you decide *right now*, with who you are, you deserve fun? Listen up. I'm going to share with you the key everyone has been looking for. You simply make the choice.

Like most great truths, this one may be overlooked because it is quite vanilla, unpretentious. Do not let the simplicity of this truth fool you into thinking it is not effective. Making a conscious decision to be happy right now, regardless what you might be facing in your personal life, can and will change your life forever. You could stop reading right here, and what I have shared with you in this paragraph could change the course of your life. (I hope you don't. There is still lots of good stuff to come.)

If you obey all the rules, you miss all the fun.
~ Katherine Hepburn

No matter what is happening in your life right now, you deserve to have fun. When your computer won't boot up, filling out your bankruptcy paperwork, or standing over your smoking car on a freeway overpass, you can choose to make it fun. Turn it into a crusade! Celebrate its shitty-ness and laugh about it.

Don't get me wrong. I'm not talking about the dreaded Pollyanna syndrome, where everything that's bad is really good, all sunshine and rainbows. I'm not suggesting you have to be happy about being laid off or losing your house. These things suck. What I'm suggesting is that fun is a choice, a decision you make. It's an agreement with your higher self to not allow external circumstances to break your spirit.

Nothing in the world is more important than being in touch with your higher self, the part of you that is linked to universal truth, the part of you that is love, elation, compassion, and understanding. In that connection lies your answers. How cool is it that the only thing you need to do to access all that groovy, wonderful stuff is to feel good now! What an amazing Universe! I love it here.

Play. Have fun. Enjoy the game.

I also give myself permission to try new things. I recently went to the drag races for the first time. It was a blast. Driving NASCAR. It was so empowering for me. Yes, I really did drive NASCAR. I can't tell you what a rush it was stepping out of my comfort zone. If I can drive NASCAR, I can do anything!

I have drafted my Le Liste, or what others may call their Bucket List, to infuse my life with fun. My list is a smidgen different than a Bucket List in, one, it has a better name. Bucket List sounds to me like I'm going fishing or something... yuck! And, my Le Liste is not about just trying to knock things off of my list before I die. It's about being alive, present, here in the moment, and fully, jubilantly living my life! Le Liste is all about flirtations, happy, fun, glee, and love.

I write down everything I want to try before I miss my chance. My Le Liste has become my blueprint for the life I want to live. At the end of this chapter, you will find instructions on how to formulate your own Le Liste. After all, what could it hurt to try it? What is that old saying? *Try it, you'll like it.*

Right now, this minute, make a decision. Even though you are not perfect, even though it's 2:00 p.m. and you are still in your pajamas, even though you have $11.00 in your checking account, even though you think Ben and Jerry's is a health food, even though your thighs have a closer relationship with each other than you do with another human being, decide you love and respect yourself enough to make the choice to have fun. Well done! The Universe and I thank you.

Check it out! This is me doing one of the items on my Le Liste, stand-up comedy! It was so much fun, and guess what? I have been asked to go back to do more stand-up! How cool is that? You never know where your Le Liste will take you. http://www.youtube.com/watch?v=-fp-wMoL5Bo

Finding Time for Fun

At the beginning of this chapter you learned about Dr. Holden and his experiment about how we don't believe we are worthy of fun and happiness. If you are going to move from fear to fun; you must ease up, have faith in your love, grasp the authentic being of wonder and brilliance you really are. I believe in you. I believe you are the beacon the world needs to see.

Now for your second homework assignment. Get out your fancy colored pen because we are going to fashion your Le Liste and identify your Top Five Passions.

Worksheets for Chapter Two
Worksheet A: Creating Your Le Liste

Let's find out how to diagram your own personal Le Liste. I have also given you other suggestions to turn your *someday I'll do* file into supreme achievements and unforgettable memories.

1. Prepare. Buy yourself an appealing journal specifically for this purpose, one that makes you happy just by looking at it. This is your Le Liste journal. Having a hard copy of your Le Liste is essential. Not only will it help you remember everything you want to accomplish (or have accomplished, I'll get to that in a minute), keeping your Le Liste handy will allow you to jot down an idea when it strikes your fancy.

> *One must work and dare*
> *if one really wants to live.*
> ~ Vincent Van Gogh

2. Plan. Everyone's got some sort of list floating around in their heads, and it's unique to every individual. I know it sounds daunting to sit down and really think about everything you want to do. Unless you start your Le Liste, will you ever accomplish everything you want to encounter? What are those things you have said over the years you want to try? Remember, there is no time limit. This is your forever to-do list. Don't limit yourself because of money or where in the world you are physically at this moment. Let your mind soar up to the heavens.

A few items on my list? Learn to sing, get a tattoo, learn to belly dance, take yoga, and ride on an elephant.

> *Each person must live their life as a model for others.*
> ~ Rosa Parks

3. Write. Now it's time to write it all down. No more procrastinating. There is great clout in putting something on paper. This sends a compelling intention to the Universe that you want this thing. Then, the Universe conspires with you for your success. Forces unseen step in to make your wish a reality. Don't spend a single second worrying about how it's going to happen. Live in the faith that you know it's coming!

Write down everything that comes into your head, as impossible as it may seem. Once you start writing your ideas down, you'll notice how they keep flowing.

We spend most of our lives
conjugating three verbs:
to want, to have, and to do.
~ Evelyn Underhill

4. Dive Right In. Every week, do one thing off of your Le Liste. No excuses! If something on your list is too big, break it down into manageable, bite-sized pieces. For example, I wanted to learn to sing, but I didn't have time for months of training. When I asked myself what it was about learning to sing that made me the happiest, it wasn't about singing like Pavarotti. I wanted to be on stage and belt out the lyrics to one of my favorite Jana Stanfield songs.

So, I did that. I got a few girlfriends together. Put on a recording of the song, then had them record a video of me singing my heart out in my living room. I fulfilled the wish of performing a song and overcame my dread of singing in front of people. I had a great time and a wonderful afternoon though I was definitely out of my comfort zone.

What can you do to break down the items on your Le Liste so you may have the situation right now? Want to buy a yacht? How about walking the marina to window-shop? Want to host your own talk show? Find two interesting people, set up the digital camera you got for Christmas, interview these folks in your living room, and post the interviews on YouTube. It worked for Justin Bieber! The most marvelous things happen when you put yourself out there. You can do this! I believe in you. Go for it!

Ninety-five percent of the failures come from the people who have the habit of making excuses.
~ George Washington Carver

5. Keep It Up. Since I started my Le Liste, I have completed about one-third of the items on my list. When fun becomes a priority, it's astonishing how exciting our days become. So far, I have gotten a tattoo, preformed stand-up comedy, volunteered at a non-profit, visited a mission, and learned to sing.

I love looking at my Le Liste to see what I can do today, this week, or this month and have it be just for me. I get to feed and nurture my soul with occurrences that elate me. In turn, I send out positive energy to everyone I meet all day. That is one substantial way to give back to the Universe. One human being joined to their source is more valuable than a million who are not. And, if we're talking about one extraordinary, spicy female who is unified with her source? Well, stand back world, things are about to change!

Keep your list and add to it consistently. Use it to dream and get excited about life again. Whenever I complete one, I place a star beside it, because I have reached for the stars... and achieved it. It's important not to start your Le Liste over. I keep a running Le Liste and I add to it all the time. Of course, as I *star* things on my list, I can also reflect back on what I've accomplished.

I feel successful because I have starred so many thrilling escapades. Whether it's driving NASCAR, performing stand-up comedy, or completing a 5-day detox, I did it!

No matter how big or small, each week you are to complete one task from your Le Liste. Think of it as training yourself to have fun again.

The principle of life is that life responds by corresponding;
your life becomes the thing you have decided it shall be.
~ Raymond Charles Barker

Keep in mind it is safe out there. I will be with you every step of the way. You've got this!

Worksheet B: The Passion Test

Did you know living a passionate life is essential to your happiness…as well as to your success? Are you living a passionate life? Take an assessment at www.karenrudat.com.

Answer seven questions to see if you're living a passionate life, to learn what you can do to feel more fulfilled. If you're ready to dive in to reveal your top five passions, contact Karen Rudat by phone at (303) 960-7439 to set up a free 30-minute consultation. Be sure to say Tara sent you.

Karen Rudat, Empowerment Coach
www.karenrudat.com

CHAPTER THREE

From Fear to Flame

How do I talk to the man I'm falling in love with about my needs, wants, and desires for my life and the relationship without scaring him off? Hell, how do I talk to him about anything at all without being scared he'll run for the hills? Maybe it's best to scare him off early so I can quit wasting my time. Why does the relationship need to be on his timeframe, anyway?

I do believe when you have given someone your heart, it is natural to want to see it through. Surely, he has come into your life for a reason.

I must admit I prefer to write my thoughts out before I share them, as I am a complete chicken when it comes to voicing my thoughts out loud (except when I have been drinking). Being rejected isn't fun, especially for those of us who have been hurt, which I expect is quite a few of us. I would think men would understand about rejection. However, they get rejection over with early, for the most part, before their heart is involved.

Last year, the guy who I was dating and I went to Las Vegas for his niece's wedding. It was the first time I had met his relatives, and naturally, I was nervous. At the reception following the ceremony, he introduced me and then ignored me for the rest of the night. For the majority of the evening, he stood on the other side of the room. He didn't hold my hand or even stand next to me. I freaked out. I couldn't think what I had done to upset him. Why wasn't he acknowledging me? My whole evening was ruined. I didn't want to be a big baby about the whole thing. I tried to be a mature, intelligent woman and wait for him to come to me. Needless to say, the whole trip was a complete disaster for me.

I allowed my mind to invent all of these elaborate stories about what I had done to him, and I held fifty arguments with him in my head. It was crazy! I was so distressed that, while driving in my car down the strip, I burned rubber on Las Vegas Boulevard.

Falling in love and having a relationship
are two different things.

Eventually, I had so much energy and steam built up around that event I exploded.

A few weeks later, I called him on the phone and demanded an explanation. "Why didn't you talk to me? What was going on? Do you hate me? If you don't want to be together, tell me!"

Oh, boy. I went off on the poor guy. He had no idea what I was talking about. The entire episode was a mystery to him. Once I calmed down and let him talk, I realized he had absolutely no idea he had neglected me that evening. He stated if I was feeling ignored, I should have gone up to him at the time, taken his hand, and asked him what the deal was.

Ugh! Curse him for having the optimal solution to my problem! What was I thinking? Here I had been suffering for weeks, thinking my relationship was in tatters, and he had no clue anything was wrong. That's because nothing was wrong. I had made the whole thing up in my head. I have now learned not to wait to ask for what I want. Chances are I will get whatever it is quickly if I only ask. Which leads me superbly to the first *thing* about relationships: communication.

Assumptions are the termites of relationships.

Face it. Stop fighting it. Men and women think differently. Our brains work differently. Men have waffle brains. They can easily compartmentalize their lives, like those squares in a waffle, all neat and organized with everything in its place, where one thing is completely separate from the other.

Women, on the other hand, have spaghetti brains. Our thought process is one long stream of consciousness, with everything relating to everything else.

Meredith Brooks explains so well
about how complicated women are in *Bitch*
http://www.youtube.com/watch?v=_ivt_N2Zcts

As nurturers and caregivers, it used to be important for women to see the inner connectedness to all things. For men, as hunters, keeping the important details, such as how not to get eaten by a lion, orderly and separate from all the other noise in their head was pretty valuable.

B.I.T.C.H.
Boldly Intending To Create Harmony

Because men have waffle brains, or are single-focused, they do one thing at a time. They're committed. They put all their attention on that one thing. When a woman asks a man a question, if he's listening to her and not already focused on something else, which is a separate issue, he commits himself to answering that question. He takes it seriously. He goes hunting for the best answer to her question. That takes time.

A re-phrased question interrupts his search for the answer to the original question. Now he's got to give up his commitment to the first and commit to the second question. That takes time, too. While he's doing that, she starts on multiple choice. By then, he's been interrupted at least twice, which is aggravating to his single-focus way of thinking. Plus, her multiple-choice options usually come from her world, not his, and are, therefore, way off the mark. That makes him think he's got no chance at this. She doesn't really care what he thinks, so he gives up altogether.

We have a strange and wonderful relationship.
He's strange and I'm wonderful.

Open your mind and listen. Be patient and don't interrupt. Since men are single-focus creatures, if they have to defend themselves, they cannot simultaneously defend the woman they would otherwise have gladly protected. In other words, they cannot defend her because they must first defend themselves from her. Then, she is left on her own.

A line from a movie called *We Bought a Zoo* goes like this, *"It's easy to communicate with girls. All you have to do is listen, they'll tell you everything."* Sometimes I need to communicate about what I'm afraid of and what I'm excited about. However, I'm never sure when it's safe to divulge these thoughts and feelings because I'm scared I'll frighten men off.

Most women are emotional and passionate. I hate it when men say women have a mental disorder or that it's that time of the month. No one wants to be labeled. If I were accepted and heard to begin with, I could move on, and it would be over. I am emotional and passionate. I want to be myself and feel free to express all my needs and wants. I want to be open and honest about everything with the man in my life. My hope for my relationship is we can be best friends as well as lovers.

Don't marry someone you can live with.
Marry someone you can't live without.

A perfect example of the difference between the male brain and the female brain is this. I once wrote an exceptionally long text to the man I was falling in love with about how important open communication was to me. I thought we needed to be honest with each other, tell each other what was going on, not hold grudges, keep open lines of communication, each speak our mind, and tell each other how we really felt about all things.

I waited with great anticipation for his response. Can you guess what his response was? Not *okay*, simply *"K"*.

I had a similar situation with my dad. I sent him an email explaining how I was sorry we were not closer and I thought our relationship could be better. I told him I was sorry I had been so distant and I was going to make an effort to get closer to him to build a better relationship. He replied with two words, *"We're okay"*.

You get it. Men are not trying to be difficult. They are actually trying to be supportive and helpful; they just think differently. And, if you want to have a great relationship with a man, you are going to have to learn to speak *man*. An expert on the subject of speaking *man* is Alison Armstrong.

Treasure your relationships, not your possessions.

Both men and women are trying to communicate with brains that come from the Stone Age. We have ancient brains geared for hunting and gathering. Back a bajillion years ago, men hunted and returned either emptyhanded or with the fruits of their labor, saving the tribe from starvation. Later, to entertain the tribe, to teach valuable lessons, and to convey important specifics, the men told the story of the hunt.

When telling a story, a man relives a particularly vivid threat or accomplishment. Through the telling the story, he may be teaching a moral lesson, proving the value of a method, encouraging others, or feeding himself with the hormones that telling the story causes to surge in his body. It is a way of recovering the energy spent in the hunt. A man will repeat the story a thousand times until the stimulus is gone or until the next hunt replaces the stimulation of the first.

Women can be hunters. But, estrogen shapes the brain more for gathering and tending. There is not nearly the same danger, provocation, or charge in gathering as there is in hunting. However, there is an enormous amount of wisdom and discernment that goes into that basket with the fruits and nuts. Upon returning from a meadow, a gatherer relays to other members of her tribe relevant and beneficial knowledge. She expects others to listen and retain it. To repeat herself would be to insult their intelligence or their memory, the same as she would be insulted. So how does a gatherer communicate with a hunter?

Speak Your Mind...But Do It Nicely

Speak your mind when in a relationship but do it in a certain way. You can make up in your mind what you think might be happening, get your facts straight first. Make sure you know what's going on before you let your subconscious run wild with an idiotic story. Remember Vegas?

According to Todd Creager, marriage and couples' therapist and author, first you have to stop arguing and agree to tell your partner honestly what is on your mind, to share with him or her the same way you'd like them to share with you.

Second, you can't just blurt it out, whatever it is you'd like to talk about. You wouldn't like it if someone punched you in the arm for no reason. This is what you are doing, verbally and emotionally, when you lie in wait for your partner with a problem or an issue and demand he go from zero to sixty in a nanosecond to suddenly be on the same page as you. Give him time to catch up to you. Let him know what's wrong or what concerns you and that you would like to talk about it in the near future.

List of Communication Don'ts

- Tell your partner you are disappointed in him
- Attack him
- Blame him for everything wrong in your life
- Argue in public
- Assume you are always right

List of Communication Dos

- Give him time
- Speak to him directly, don't assume
- Be nice
- Let him be right once in a while

Would you rather be happy or be right?

Let's face it, ladies, isn't the objective for you to be able to communicate with your man in a way you get what you need and want from him? Am I right? In my generation, women have adopted a behavior that has translated into emasculating our men. Don't get me started on why it happened or how it started, because it doesn't matter. What does matter is that it's taught our men we don't need them. This counterproductive approach to how women handle relationships needs to be rectified. We keep treating them like they are women. This is our first mistake! Men and women are different. We think differently, play different roles in human interaction. Men generally do one thing at a time (waffle brain). If they are watching the game, they will never see the garbage that needs to be taken out. EVER! So, don't nag. The trash really doesn't need to be taken out before the end of the fourth quarter with 30 seconds on the clock and the basketball game is tied. I recommend waiting. Then, when you ask, ask in a manner that he would be proud to dispose of the trash. (It's not your fault if you're berating yourself with self-talk right now.) We have been trained to behave in this manner, and you are not the only one. As I mentioned earlier, I can say with certainty that a large percentage of the baby boomer generation of women has a propensity to exhibit this behavior. You are also not the only woman the men in your life are dealing with where they are the recipient of emasculative behavior.

I highly recommend the work of Alison Armstrong, author of *The Queen's Code*, who speaks about "frog farming" and why we do it. In short, it is women's knee-jerk response to how we have learned to deal with our hurt, disappointment, and frustration. There are great steps that help us work toward replacing our unproductive behavior with the more effective language of men. Men want to be our heroes, and we need to create the space so they can be.

I have taken Ms. Armstrong's vow to quit treating men as if they are misbehaving and deserve to be punished. I made the choice to take her oath, since then, it's been great. Nothing is that important to be upset about anymore. I no longer tell any man in any situation, from my current boyfriend to the man at the hardware store that I'm needing his assistance, how to respond. I show them the upmost respect and ask for what I need. It's taken some time and I'm still perfecting my skills.

I've noticed how I tend to get what I want more often in the way I need it when I use the language of men.

Forgiveness is a Verb

In my opinion, forgiveness is unconditional love. It is the foundation of healthy relationships. We want to hold onto being right when we have been wronged. To forgive is a form of gratitude. When you forgive someone and let go of *I've been wronged*, you can turn that circumstance into gratitude. By forgiving, you open up the space to love them and see the real them. You begin to replace your anger and disappointment with gratitude.

Humanity Healing on the Power of Forgiveness
http://www.youtube.com/watch?v=erqJF_ppqbk

If you release the anger and have the intention of replacing it with love and gratitude, you will live a better life.

You've got to be ready to be in a great relationship.

When you choose not to forgive, and it is a choice, the only person you hurt is yourself. Half the time the other person doesn't even know you are mad at them. The health problems are yours, not theirs. You suffer, not them.

Don't choose the better guy.
Choose the guy who makes you the better girl.

The importance of forgiveness in a relationship cannot be overstated. Part of learning to live in the now is allowing your partner to be better than he was before. By forgiving him, you allow him to be a better person today and overcome his past. Do you want to be judged as the person you were five or ten years ago? Nah. I didn't think so. So, stop holding a grudge.

The question I ask myself about the man in my life is: Would I rather have him in my life with his issues or not have him in my life? I definitely would have wanted him in my life. He had many great qualities that I never gave him credit for. I can see that now. I am now learning to see the whole person and not judge, accepting him for who he is, as I hope to be accepted for who I am.

No partner in a love relationship should feel
that she has to give up an essential part of herself
to make the relationship viable.

Energy Bookmarks

Imagine moving on from an unfulfilling relationship with grace and dignity. Allow me to share the idea behind an energy bookmark. Everything is energy and each of us is energy, correct? A dazzling ball of energy. When I have someone in my life, I take on their energy, or more specifically, hold a place for them in my life, like a bookmark.

If you continue to be with anyone who isn't right for you or who may not even be in your life anymore, you hold yourself away from the person who *is* right for you. Are you holding on to the hope your husband or old boyfriend is coming back? Open up and allow the space in your life where the right person is supposed to fit that is currently being held by the wrong person. The wrong person is using up that energy bookmarked for your relationship, so, your new guy can't come along until that space is free. Make sense? As long as you are holding onto someone who isn't right for you, the right person will not be able to find you.

Forgive the wrong person, move on, and let them go. Open up that energy bookmark, to let your soulmate be drawn to you.

Loving You Five Different Ways

Another language I'd like to touch on is love language. One of the most influential books I have ever read about relationships is *The Five Love Languages* by Gary Chapman. Chapman introduces us to the idea that we grow up with our own love language. By speaking our love language to us, we know we are loved. This is a biggie when it comes to communication and being clear. If you and your partner do not speak the same love language, each of you will be confused, even think you are not loved by the other.

Do your relationship a favor. Check out *The Five Love Languages*. If nothing else, it'll clue you in on more information about yourself.

A quick overview of *The Five Love Languages*
http://www.youtube.com/watch?v=aQsBwRrbS78

I know I've been talking about relationships with other people, primarily a love partner. What I don't want you to miss out on is your relationship with yourself. If you don't love yourself, how could anyone else love you? This is the message you could be putting out into the Universe. Loving yourself does a lot of things. It makes you whole so you are not looking to a relationship to fill up any emptiness within yourself. Also, confidence and self-esteem are the best aphrodisiacs for any relationship.

I personally was always waiting for someone to love me like I wanted to be loved. What I realized is why do I have to wait for someone else to love me the way I want to be loved? So, I decided to have a love affair with myself. Be my own best friend. What I do now is write love letters, letters of encouragement, and greeting cards. I then mail myself these cards and letters.

I have purchased beautiful stationery and fun pens. I have also sent myself amazing greeting cards. Either way, I address them then, send them to myself in the mail. By sending them in the mail, it solidifies the thoughts and sends a message to the Universe. When was the last time you received a pretty card with just the right message on it? I can't tell you how many times I've sent myself cards. Then, when I received them, it was the perfect support statement I needed for what was going on that day.

For a time, I was sending myself greeting cards on a regular basis. Shopping for greeting cards is a bit of an obsession of mine. It's quite normal for me to come home with a bag full of cards. It was especially dangerous at those Hallmark stores. Remember those?

At one point, I was sending and receiving at least one card a week. I mixed them up. I didn't know which card to expect. There is divine timing in this process because I was having a really bad day and the card that arrived in my mailbox was perfect! Let me take a moment to tell you about it. The front of the card read: Be Brave Be Kind Be True Be You. The inside was scribed in my handwriting and read as follows: "Tara, know you can count on me to be in your corner. I am your loudest cheerleader and your biggest supporter. Whatever you need, I am here to help you get it. Love, Me."

To receive this after going through the postal service and landing in my mailbox, what an impact it had on me. This is why I am encouraging you to try this exercise. The results can truly be amazing!

Go to the end of this chapter for instructions on starting your own personal love affair with yourself. I also love flowers! Hint, hint to self.

Worksheets for Chapter Three
Worksheet A: Creating Your Evidence Journal

Yes, you are going to need a journal. You could use one journal for all your works. I prefer using separate journals (and pens) of the decorative design. For some reason, their appearance lures me into using them. It's up to you.

The purpose of this journal will be to record when you've changed your behavior toward your partner. It's also very important to record your partner's response to your behavior. I find it easier to do this daily instead of trying to remember every time at the end of the week. If you're able to record them when they happen, that would be ideal. Otherwise, take a few minutes before you go to sleep to notate that day's events. Our goal is to have you be a winner at treating your man with the respect he deserves, which, in turn, will allow him to treat you the way you want and deserve. Start recording your evidence.

Worksheet B: Love Letters

You guessed it! You are going to start to express love to yourself through writing. The first assignment is to write yourself a letter. If it were me, I would start with nice stationery and pens. Use the salutation that reflects how you'd like to be addressed, "Dear ____". Then, take at least 10 minutes to tell yourself things you'd like someone else to tell you. Things you really need to hear! Write it down, especially if it feels strange. Take more time if you'd like. Say as many wonderful things as you can think of to yourself. Because that is the idea. If you're an artist, images are nice although words have a lot more impact on us. Last but not least, you need to put the letter in the envelope, address it to yourself, put postage on the letter, now actually mail it. As I mentioned earlier, there is much power in sending through the mail. Send me your address and I'll send you one, too!

CHAPTER FOUR

From Fear to Fabulous

Our deepest fear is not that we are inadequate. Our deepest fear is that we are powerful beyond measure. It is our light, not our darkness, that most frightens us. We ask ourselves who am I to be brilliant, gorgeous, talented, fabulous? Actually, who are you not to be? You are a child of God. You're playing small does not serve the world. There is nothing enlightened about shrinking so that other people won't feel insecure around you. We were born to make manifest the glory of God that is within us. It is not just in some of us, it is in everyone. And as we let our own light shine, we unconsciously give other people permission to do the same. As we are liberated from our own fear, our presence automatically liberates others.

~ Marianne Williamson

If we talked to our friends the way we talk to ourselves, we would have no friends. When are we not saying horrible things about ourselves? When do we not believe the worst will happen? I do this all the time.

As I mentioned earlier, one of the things on my Le Liste was to take a stand-up comedy class. Recently, I found one that looked like a lot of fun. *What the hell? You'll never know if you don't try!* So, I signed up.

I had to miss the first class, and when I showed up for the second class, everyone was supportive and happy to see me. They laughed at all of my jokes and encouraged me. I thought I was a star. I did cartwheels. Everyone loved me!

When I showed up for the next class, however, no one laughed at my material. I was beside myself and my inner dialogue went berserk. *What is wrong with me? Why doesn't anyone like me? I suck at this. I'm not good enough. I'll never be any good at anything.* On and on it went.

I was incapacitated by self-doubt and distracted by my self-talk, I couldn't concentrate for the remainder of the class.

What you think of me is none of my business.

What's Self-Love Got To Do With It?

Looking back, I saw one of the biggest lessons I needed to learn was how to change my inner dialogue and love myself. I had become oblivious to the fact the voices in my head were not in my own best interests. It was senseless I would give careful thought to what to wear, but I never gave a second thought to what I said to myself. I wasn't paying attention to the one person I couldn't get away from. Me. Man, I was saying some irrational shit about myself.

If I had a girlfriend who spoke that way, I would ditch her as a friend on the spot. Who wants to hang out with such a negative, pessimistic, judgmental person? It was everything I didn't want in my life, and that girlfriend was me! This realization was like a bad *Twilight Zone* episode.

To change your self-talk, you need to become aware of what you are telling yourself. Then, you need to replace your degrading inner dialogue. Every time you catch yourself saying something destructive about yourself, you need to talk back. Argue with yourself. Fight for yourself. The things you are telling yourself are lies. These thoughts aren't truths. They are bad habits.

You have been saying the same thing for so long you believe it to be valid. It's not. It's familiar. But, you can start a new positive inner dialogue at any time. You are enough. You are exquisite. You have everything you need inside of you. You can form a new habit that serves you better.

It's going to be unbearable at first. Anytime you start something new, it's always awkward until it's graceful. You may try to numb the torment and stop. That's okay. Breathe and talk yourself through it. Remember, you have a choice to make. You can decide to move through it or go back to your old ways. If you move through it at some point, it won't be as much a struggle the next time.

In the blink of an eye, you could be through it and living the life you have always pictured. This new way of being will be your new habit. How cool is that? However, if you do choose to stay in your old patterns, I can almost guarantee you will stay in agony. Nothing will change. If I can do it, so can you. I am with you every step of the way. I love you. I believe in you.

Insanity: Doing the same thing over and over again
and expecting different results.

Let's pitch your negative self-talk, or your *head trash*. Did you know the majority of the convictions you hold were established before you were three years old? How you feel about yourself, about the world, and about your relationships.

I don't know about you, I can't even remember being three, let alone what was going on in the world and my family at that time. Why should I be limited by beliefs that were imprinted on my brain when I was a toddler? How ridiculous!

These beliefs don't serve me in any way now. Replacing them with more positive, affirming beliefs means I spend my time in a more productive way, which has changed my life in the most unexpected ways.

I'm looking to feel special
because I've never really ever felt adequate.

Picture an iceberg: 5 percent is visible, while 95 percent is hidden. Our minds are similar to icebergs in that the 5 percent that is visible is your Conscious Mind and the hidden 95 percent is your Subconscious Mind. Your Subconscious Mind is like a totally dark room. When you can't see something, it's awfully hard to change it. To make lasting change, you need to change your Subconscious Mind. Clearing your head trash lets you quiet the chatter of your Conscious Mind and access your Subconscious Mind.

When you clear your head trash, you give others permission to clear theirs, too. This is how we all become more of who we really are.

The ABCs To Clear Your Head Trash:

A. Awareness. Being aware of what you say to yourself is key to this process. Every time you start to drift away from the present moment, bring yourself back. In the beginning, your mind may stray a thousand times a day. That's okay. Keep bringing yourself back. It will get easier. Awareness is the first step. Once you have taken notice of this awareness, give yourself grace that you actually noticed you were not in the present moment and almost or perhaps did get in a few "digs" of your negative self-talk, which could have spiraled you down to the Ben & Jerry's lane to Crunchy Monkey. But it didn't. Kudos to you!

B. Breathe. Take the next moment or two to take a long, deep breath. While breathing, I concentrate on the feeling of gratitude. Be grateful that you are now aware and can make the necessary corrections. Really take in the feeling of gratitude. (We'll talk about gratitude in more depth later.)

C. Choose. Choose a different story, because you are worth it. Yes, there is a price to pay, because you will feel uncomfortable. Only you can decide if it's worth it. You already know how it feels to stay stuck or repeat your old patterns. Life is short, do you want who you are now to be your legacy? We have the opportunity, every second of every day, to change ourselves and choose the life we were meant to live. The price we pay is a bit of discomfort as we build new habits and new beliefs. That is not a bad deal. Create your new story and feel it. Spend time every day practicing being the person you want to be. I've said it before, practice makes permanent. What thoughts would you have? How would you walk? How would you talk to people? What would you do with your day? Sitting in traffic or standing in line at the supermarket is the perfect time to practice. From Dr. Holden, just start with one minute a day. You'll find how easy it is to add more time daily.

Afformations

No, that's not a typo. Afformations are a brainchild I discovered that literally saved my life. If you have tried affirmations in the past and have not seen the results you were hoping for, you might want to give Afformations a try.

A few years back, a smart guy, Neal St. John, uncovered that the brain and the Subconscious Mind are natural problem-solvers and respond better to questions than they do to statements. Our minds are constantly sorting through billions of bits of data, putting the puzzle pieces together, and finding us the answers we seek.

Neal decided to turn his affirmations from statements into positive questions that the Subconscious could work to find answers to. For example, instead of saying, *I am wealthy*, he asked, *Why am I wealthy? Why do I attract so much wealth quickly and easily?*

Get it? Can you feel the difference in your energy when you ask a question? You can feel your Subconscious going to work to find the answer to your question and bring you wealth. Wording your affirmation as a positive question also guarantees you are focusing on what you're yearning for instead of on the lack of whatever it is you are pursuing. You are attracting what you want instead of the opposite of what you want. I have given you a few more examples to get you started:

Why am I always lucky?
Why do I get to have all I go after?
Why am I always surrounded by the most uplifting people?
Why do I radiate fun and love?
Why does my body heal quickly?
Why am I able to lose weight quickly and effortlessly?

I am wonderful as I am.
I have so much to offer and so many gifts to share.

Stop Picking on Yourself Already

Enough. You're not perfect, and neither is anyone else, so give yourself a break. It's time to stop all of that. Even celebrities and models who have been stamped with the media's perfect-body seal of approval have things they dislike about themselves. They have not been blessed with excessive amounts of high self-esteem, either! I am, right now, giving you permission to be imperfect and love your body just the way it is.

Take care of your body.
It is the only place you have to live.

I'm going to let you in on a concept that helped me to finally achieve the body I have always coveted and allowed me to love my body unconditionally. In order to change your body, you have to accept it as it is right now. You have to accept the fact you are perfect as you are and are worth taking care of. As long as you despise yourself, you won't be able to make any lasting changes to your life or your body. Why would you take care of something you hate?

I know this sounds counterintuitive. You look in the mirror and think there is nothing perfect about your body, but it is the very attachment to that idea that keeps you stuck. Your focus is on the wrong thing and is preventing you from being at peace with yourself to achieve the results you want.

Embracing yourself just as you are
will free you to become
the person you have always wanted to be.

Your Body is Your Temple

Suppose wanting to build a house and hating the raw materials that were dropped off. The lumber is warped, the sheetrock is broken, the colors are hideous, and the fixtures are the ugliest you've ever seen. Now, you're being told you have to build your dream house out of these materials. You can't do it. You can't build your dream house out of icky components you hate. How far do you think you'll get before you give up?

The Inner Weigh Coaches talk about
loving your body just as it is
http://www.youtube.com/watch?v=ByZdA6DybUc

The body you currently have is your raw material. It is from this material you are trying to build your dream body. Every time you stand in front of the mirror and criticize your body, you remind yourself you can't build the body you want because you're not enough. You are enough, you are more than enough, and you can yield the body you want from where you are right now. You aren't going to get any more raw material to work with. What you've got now is it. Honor and love the parts you have been given. They are going to carry you forward into the life you want.

I am not saying you have to resign yourself to your current shape and size. What I am saying is you have to stop fighting yourself. You have to be willing to lose a battle or two to win the war. It all starts with you loving yourself right here, right now.

From this day forward, when you look in the mirror, I want you to praise yourself and your body. *This is my raw material. This is my extraordinary body, and it is worth loving. I am perfect as I am. From where I stand right now, I can work with my body to lovingly bring forth a fitter, healthier, happy me.*

*What do you think could be accomplished in the world
if women took just 10 percent of the time they spent
hating their bodies and put that into healing the world?
World peace. That's what would happen!*

I'm just saying, give your thighs a break, and go solve some problems! Can we put that on a bumper sticker?

Just *57* Percent... That's Sad

As I browsed one of my favorite blogs, a reader poll pertaining to body image appeared on the homepage. I cannot tell you how many times a day I run into people who carry around an unhealthy amount of shame and self-loathing toward their bodies. This guilt and negativity can and will contaminate every part of your life, from the clothes you put on in the morning to your sex life, from your feelings of acceptance and happiness in your job and friendships to your relationship with yourself.

Learning to love yourself regardless of your size
is one of the most crucial and beneficial gifts
a person can give themselves.

The ripple effects of learning to love yourself will touch every part of your life. The poll asked, *When I look at myself naked in the mirror, I feel...* How would you answer that question? Believe it or not, 57 percent of women answered they felt shame. Now, I am no stranger to feeling ashamed of my body. It broke my heart that many other people shared the same sentiment.

The most startling thing about this problem is it affects people equally who have a myriad of different body types and sizes. Almost everyone, no matter how skinny, how tall, or how perfectly shaped, feels this way about themselves from time to time. It is important to promote healthy body image regardless of size, even when that seems difficult.

This is the one and only body we've been given this lifetime. Start treating it with the love and tenderness it deserves. What is it you are telling yourself about your body? Are you berating yourself in front of your full-length mirror? What beliefs do you have about your body?

Notice if any of the phrases you tell yourself came from other people's idea of what you "should" look like. This could be the media, your family, your parents, or your friends. The reason I mention this is you came into this world with no preconceived notions about anything, especially the opinion of how you look. These ideas are beliefs that you have taken on as your truth. It's time you started loving your body avatar.

Nutrition is one area of focus. Research what foods work best with your body metabolism. There are numerous books written on the subject of nutrition and diet. Begin by feeding your body the food it needs to thrive. This will assist with any weight loss if that is one of your goals.

The other is exercise. It's a balancing act between exercise and the food we consume. I've experienced that food is about 80% of the equation to reaching the body goals I've set for myself, leaving exercise the remaining 20%. Regardless, we need to consume the amount of calories equal to the number of calories burned just to maintain our current weight. This means, in order to shed pounds, we need to eat fewer calories than we burn. Capiche?

I strive to eat the foods my body can easily metabolize in order to give me energy without any of that sluggishness I feel after eating such items as fried foods, dairy, sugar, or gluten. Please know I do splurge now and again. Instead of calling them splurges though, I call them rewards. For instance, on my personal nutrition food plan when I keep to my food regime with no slip-ups after 4 days, I have earned an extra credit to indulge in one reward. Sometimes, it's a glass of champagne.

My exercise plan is also custom-based on what my body likes along with the exercise that fits me. Right now I'm walking mostly. The walk is a brisk walk with my wonderful golden retriever, Cinnamon. I continue to research and try new forms of exercise to determine what I prefer. Next on my list to try is cardio barre. This is my personal plan just for me. I'm customizing it to suit my needs. Because I love my body and want to treat it with the love and tenderness it deserves.

Let's go back to food. As a reminder, food is 80% of the equation. I'm not sure if you've experienced this before, I've found, sometimes, I am eating my feelings. I notice it's when I'm having a negative feeling (BTW – I'm having one right now when I'm writing this sentence). Eating was a way to cope with my negative feelings in order to rid myself of the feeling. Or, so I thought. However, the feeling may subside temporarily, and eating is not the cure. It only places a bandage on it until the negative feeling rears its ugly head the next time. Can you see how eating my feelings may have contributed to weight gain?

Keeping a food journal was a great way I was able to notice what I was eating every day. I was sure to also include any beverages including water. Hydration is another component of my plan. I started drinking anywhere from 1/3 to 1/2 my body weight in ounces. A trick I found was, if I drink water, it reduces my appetite. That way I eat less because I feel full. Again, I only eat when I'm hungry and determine the real reason for my eating. This may sound daunting at first. This is a great research project to see not only what and how much you are eating but why you are eating.

Before you take that first bite, ask yourself *Am I hungry? Why am I hungry* or *What am I hungry for?* Be sure to note this in your food journal. Also notice what you are telling yourself. What thoughts or beliefs are coming up for you right now? Are you telling yourself any garbage? This is a great way to learn what your triggers are and why you may be overeating or feeding yourself "junk food" to fill up your emotions.

One piece that is often forgotten is sleep. A full night's sleep restores and heals. It is irreplaceable for optimal physical, mental, and emotional performance. Check to see you're getting an adequate amount of sleep each night.

A situation I needed to deal with was adrenal fatigue because I wasn't getting enough sleep. My internal sleep clock was out of whack. I sought help from a professional. Since my diagnosis, I have treated the problem and am back on track with my internal sleep clock. My sleep plan is to make sure I get at least 7 hours of sleep each night. That's my number. What's yours?

With our crazy schedules, computers, smart phones, tablets, we are *on* all the time. It's important to *unplug* from time to time to regroup and just be with ourselves. I often take this time when I'm walking my dog and notice the world around me without my cell phone. Dine on the patio with only music playing and no interruptions. Turn off the television, silence the cell phone, stay off the computer. I take time to be with myself and people I like to spend time with.

All these steps are you taking care of you. If not you, then who? You must take care of yourself first. Just like the flight attendant instructs us on inflight safety procedure – put your oxygen mask on first!

Check in with yourself to see what your body is telling you and remember your body has all the answers. You just need to be quiet enough to hear it. When you listen to your body, it will provide you with the answers you're seeking. Trust it!

Love your body like Jana Stanfield sings about in *Hottie*
http://www.youtube.com/watch?v=D4GVvF8KP6g

Tools for Learning to Love Your Body No Matter What Your Size:

- **Buy clothing that fits you.** Buy pretty things that allow you to feel comfortable, striking, and pulled together. Don't even look at the size on the label. Buying clothes that don't fit is a form of self-abuse. Stop it! Not only is this a subtle way of reminding yourself, all day long, you are not okay, it also isn't fooling anyone. It doesn't make you look smaller or leaner, it only makes you look uncomfortable. Buy what makes you feel really good.

- **Talk sweetly to yourself.** Look in the mirror and tell yourself how lovely you look. Extra credit if you can do this naked. Because, remember, you are fetching.
- **Dismiss the evil-doers.** Do not give people who delight in making you feel fat, ugly, unlovable, or unworthy a single second of your time. Wash your hands of them. Have compassion for them if you can, because the root of their meanness probably lies in their own insecurities.
- **Move your body.** It is harder to hate your body when you move it. You will feel better with every step you take – yoga, walking, swimming, dancing – it doesn't matter. Just move. Consider doing something outside. Most of us are terribly deficient in Vitamin D. Twenty minutes in the sun lets you soak up those golden rays and will elevate your mood.
- **Do not sit around with your friends, family, or loved ones and bitch about your body.** Moaning about your body is not an excellent form of social interaction. It hurts you. It hurts them. I am willing to bet my life you have better things to do with your time.

The Soul is the voice of the body's interests.

I'm Too Sexy
https://www.youtube.com/watch?v=39YUXIKrOFk

How to Be a Hottie

Being sensual does not mean you're a floozy. Be confident. Over the years, I have collected tips and pointers that have helped me to look and feel alluring. Let's call it my Nurture List, which I happily share with you now.

- Remember, your body is your temple. You are living in this human body. Love it, treat it with kindness, cherish it.
- Eat foods that are best for your body. If you don't know what they are, do research. Read books or consult a professional. Chances are what feels right to you will be right for you because you have all of the answers.
- Supplement the food you eat if necessary. Again, if you don't know how to do this, seek out the facts or find a nutritionist.
- Be more open-minded and less close-minded.
- Take good care of your skin with quality sunscreen and moisturizer.
- Get regular facials.
- Find a hairstyle that is currently fashionable and flattering.
- Be well rested.
- Exercise. I don't want to be in a wheelchair for the last years of my life because I didn't take care of my body. *Use it or lose it*, as they say. Exercise, even if it's just walking or yoga. Whatever you can commit to is great. Your goal is to be agile and have strong bones and muscles. When you work those muscles, you're burning fat, and strengthening your bones.
- Treat yourself to a massage on occasion or regularly if you can.
- If plastic surgery is your thing, own it, do it! Just don't overdo it. Age gracefully.
- Be proud of your accomplishments and the person you've become.
- Develop a healthy and tasteful sense of humor.
- Maintain your mystique by keeping your personal secrets.
- Become comfortable with touching and being touched.
- Maintain high standards for personal hygiene.
- Become a better kisser and revel in it more.

- Go to the theater to see romantic movies when they come out.
- Learn to talk in a more intimate way when the occasion arises.
- Luxuriate in bubble baths, candles, scented oils, and flowers.
- Purchase a racy item to wear to bed, or sleep in the nude once in a while.
- Learn the important differences between sexiness and sleaziness.
- Get your teeth cleaned and whitened so you can smile more freely.
- Feel more pleasure and spontaneity and less inhibition with sex.
- Dress in clothes that are soft and sensual to celebrate your femininity and complement your spiciness.
- Listen to music that makes you feel good.
- Learn to look people in the eyes more often.
- Wear something that makes a guy guess what's underneath.
- Save an enticing outfit for an erotic special occasion.
- Develop your ability to flirt with seductive body language.
- Become a better dancer so you can move with more grace.
- Loosen up.

Start with mine or come up with your own Nurture List.

Love, dance, laugh loudly,
and don't shy away
from shining your light.

Worksheets for Chapter Four
Worksheet A: Make Your Personal Uplifting Playlist

The rhythm of the music and dancing to the beat help me get into my body and allow me to be present and in the moment. Dancing is also great exercise. Go ahead, make your own personal music mix. Below is a list of a few songs on my playlist:

If I Were Brave by Jana Stanfield
Bring It On by Jana Stanfield
I Love Myself by Kingsand
Ready to Fly by FFH
18 Wheeler by Pink
Raise Your Glass by Pink
Reach Up by O.A.R.
Fly by Avril Lavigne
I Am Invincible by Cassadee Pope
Fight Song by Rachel Platten
Crazy in Love by Beyonce
Firework by Katy Perry
Roar by Katy Perry
Born This Way by Lady Gaga
Stronger by Kelly Clarkson
Don't Cha by The Pussycat Dolls
Believe by Cher
Shake Your Hips by Joan Osborne
Only Girl (In the World) by Rihanna
I Gotta Feeling by The Black Eyed Peas

Worksheet B: Write Down Your Personal Afformations

Affirmations are great. I highly recommend doing them. As stated earlier, I like Afformations. Let's give it a whirl. Start an Afformations list, or better yet, use a journal. Come up with as many as you can. Fill up a page. Now add another page and another. I have provided you with suggestions here to get you started:

Why am I lucky in love?
How is it I can do what I love as a career?
Why am I financially prosperous?
Why is it easy for me to maintain my ideal weight?
How did I easily find my perfect mate?
Why have I been successful in business?
How do I know how to choose the most impeccable clothes for me?

CHAPTER FIVE

From Fear to Fortune

I am wealth.
I am abundance.
I am joy.
~ David Cameron Gikandi

David Cameron Gikandi, author *of A Happy Pocket Full of Money,* explains it well. I love how he ties quantum physics and spirituality together so all you scientific individuals can now understand spirituality. He says, in fact, time doesn't really exist. It's an illusion. Your mind has tricked you into thinking time is real and you are under its control. This is because you are thinking of time as linear, which it is not. The plain truth is your life is exactly how you want it. You're just not experiencing it right now.

Abundance is not something we acquire.
It is something we tune into.

Deepak Chopra and other spiritual sages teach us that having an abundance consciousness allows us to look at our lives as a magical quest, where our needs are met with grace and ease. This quest also includes the capacity to have gratitude as our primary emotion (I will speak more on this in a bit), be open and trust in the cosmic plan. According to the Law of Intention and Desire, we identify that at the core of reality is a field of energy where all creation originates. By placing our attention on exactly what we want, bliss, love, and prosperity will manifest themselves in one's life.

The Law of Attraction actualizes your intentions and actions to produce significant change just as leverage amplifies a relatively small force to produce a relatively large result. Is anyone else getting high school physics class flashbacks? Investors use leverage when they borrow money with the expectation that the rate of return will be greater than the cost of the loan, making it possible to generate earnings even when they don't have the cash for an investment. In mechanics, leverage is produced when you push down on the long end of a stick resting on a fulcrum so the short end moves upward with great force.

Proof that the Law of Attraction works!
A trailer for the movie, *Just My Luck*
http://youtu.be/jiSiknwRGpY

A three-step process is made simple by Chris and Janet Attwood, authors of *The Passion Test.* Intention, Attention, No Tension. Envision exactly what you want. I mean exactly. This is your intention. Remember the old saying, *be careful what you wish for*? Be as specific as possible.

Then, place your attention on your intention because attention energizes and transforms. Feel your intention in the deepest parts of you. How do you look, feel, or sound when your attention is on your intention?

Now, release the tension, surrender it. Allow the Universe to work out the details for you. You don't have to worry about how or when your intention will happen. Whatever you do, don't hold on to the intention! Otherwise, the Universe cannot give your intention to you. Keep in mind I'm just like you. I'm still working on this whole process.

Gratitude Is Unconditional Appreciation, Reverence, Respect, and Joy

Many people suffer from the disease of *not-enoughness*. This comes from focusing on what they don't have, which produces more feelings of not having enough! This incredible Universe makes it easy for us to get the things we crave. If you take one tiny step toward your goal, the Universe barrels toward you like a freight train to help out. Being grateful is one of the fastest ways to tell the Universe that you want more of something. Feeling and expressing gratitude is one of the best ways to access the piggy bank of the Universe. When you feel gratitude, your ego steps aside.

To feel gratitude, consider all the wonderful things you have already faced or you already own. If you're not happy with what you have (believe it or not, you've asked for everything you already possess), why would the Universe give you anything else?

When you receive a gift, it's customary and polite to thank the giver, right? In that same vein, when you are grateful for what you have, the Universe will produce for you more of what you wish for. By giving thanks for all you have and committing to living your life in complete appreciation, riches will surely come your way. That is the attractive decree of gratitude.

Focus on what you have, not on what you lack. Appreciating your life with gratitude clears away any thought of not having enough or limitation. Gratitude is independent of the situation, circumstance, or personal event. Thinking of the many things in your life and taking stock of them is like energy currency. Keeping a gratitude journal is equal to putting money in your spiritual bank. Start one now! What are you waiting for? (Please see the end of this chapter for information about how to compose your own gratitude journal.)

Express gratitude by telling the people in your life how important they are to you. Pick up the phone, call a friend, write an email, or send a text. Better yet, send a card or letter letting them know how thankful you are for their presence in your life. Obviously, use the words that articulate your feelings. Don't let me put words in your mouth. You may be surprised to hear your friend's reaction.

You can take it one step further. Smile, greet, or say thank you to the people you come into contact with daily. The lady that walks her dog on the trail where you run. The cashier at the hardware store. The checker at the supermarket. The sky's the limit.

Finding Your Calling

When people talk about abundance, they ask a lot of questions. *What do I do with my life? How can I find work that is fulfilling and is in alignment with my higher calling?* Okay, I hear you. Let's see if I can help you out.

*Doing what you love is the cornerstone
of having abundance in your life.*

There are three essential questions you need to ask yourself when deciding on a career, profession, or business venture. They helped me refine my career path and begin trusting my own inner guidance.

1. What gives me joy? What makes my heart sing?
2. What are my unique talents? What am I best at?
3. What does the world need? How can I share my gifts to bring happiness to others?

You will need to listen. You may get many answers to these questions. If you listen closely, one of them will whisper to you that it is your calling. What I've learned is that soft whispers often lead to a delightful adventure and a life worth living. We may have hundreds of callings in our life. Each whisper gives us a chance to sample another aspect of what makes us come alive.

Career + Love + Passion = An Extraordinary Life

Do What You Love and The Money Will Follow

While most of us would love to have a career we are passionate about, finding ways to do what you love for a living also benefits both you and the world. People are terrified to start such an expedition. They think horrible things will happen. They'll end up homeless and friendless. I know I did.

Nothing could be further from the truth. Have you ever stood outside a club or a restaurant and from the street, it appeared dark, quiet, and foreboding? However, when you mustered the nerve to open the door and peek inside, the atmosphere was bright, warm, and welcoming. Then you thought, *wow, I could have walked right by and never known this spectacular place was here.*

That's more or less what doing this work and finding your calling feels like. From the outside it appears cold, dark, and lonely. However, once you find the fortitude to immerse yourself, you'll find the exact opposite to be the case.

Life in abundance comes only through great love.

I hope you have taken the time to answer these three questions because I have provided you with steps I hope will help you turn your passions into a career you will love.

Let's Look at Ten Ways to Turn Your Passion Into a Career

1. Soul searching. To do something you love, you first must spend time thinking critically about the things that bring you gratification. Take a step back. Figure out what you relish doing. Write down as many specific details as possible. Don't try to fit these details into a specific career or industry. Your dream job or business may not exist yet. By categorizing or pigeon-holing yourself too early, you shortchange yourself. Only after you come up with the list of things that illuminate you should you think about the careers that each might fit.

Check out Sue Frederick and *I See Your Dream Job*
http://iseeyourdreamjob.com/

When you don't have a clear plan, the plan has you.

2. Make time to make it happen. Nothing happens by chance. You have to make room for your new life and career to grow. These beginning steps are fragile. It is all too easy to dismiss our passions as frivolous and unimportant when they are not making us any money and not garnering any attention.

Remember both Bill Gates and Steve Jobs started out in their parents' garages, inventing products the world had never seen. Imagine the determination it must have taken to walk into that garage every night. Work on their businesses when almost no one in the world understood what they were doing. When no money was coming in, and when all their friends and family were admonishing them to be sensible and keep their day jobs.

To dream by night is to escape your life.
To dream by day is to make it happen.

It takes a lot of resolve to do this work. Honor that by carving out the time you need to nurture your new life. Make it a reality. You give time to all the other important things in your life: your partner, your children, your health. The work you do while you are on this planet deserves the same amount of consideration.

If I Were Brave by Jana Stanfield
http://www.youtube.com/watch?v=UF5V2PEujqs

Once you've determined which of your passions you want to shape into a career, it is critical to take the steps necessary to turn that idea into a reality. Once we pinpoint ideas, we need to do something about which we usually are decidedly not passionate: schedule time in our calendars to come up with our plan to get there. Make the time. I promise it will be worth it. The plan must be written down. Then broken down into baby steps.

Don't give up, ever!

3. Figure out how to profit from your passion. Of course, to turn something you love into a business, you have to determine how you will make money doing it. Spend time brainstorming.

For example, people who love art could fund their passions in several ways, such as by teaching art, working in a gallery, opening a gallery, selling their caricatures online, or painting portraits.

> *To find the best in others, to lead them to*
> *inspiration that allows them to find their gifts.*
> *Then, to inspire their gifts to bloom through*
> *encouragement and support by many caring others.*
> *Then, to provide the tools and leadership,*
> *creating the change that they can provide for the world.*
> *That is our authentic calling.*

4. Talk to others who have done it. Find others already doing what you want to do. If you spend time really talking to others in the field in which you are interested, you will uncover hidden anguish and treasure that will let you know if you are on the right track.

If you decide one of your many passions is baking cupcakes, you then spend time with the wonderful bakers in your area. You may realize the early morning hours, the hiring of staff, and doing payroll are not what you expected. Suddenly, the idea of having your own corner bakery doesn't sound too appealing. Aren't you glad you detected that before and not after you spent all your savings? Maybe you cross that one off your list and take a look at your passion for writing.

*The good kind of friend not only encourages
you to grow and inspires you to grow.
The good kind of friend makes you
believe that you can grow.*

5. Surround yourself with supportive people. You are as successful as the five people closest to you. Think about that for a second. Who are you surrounding yourself with? Do they uplift and support you, or do they drag you down, telling you that you can't do it?

Support creates momentum, instills confidence and promotes inspiration. Your support team is *your* tribe. Spend time assembling the right team to make your dreams happen. You may need to initially keep these ideas from your family and friends. Oftentimes, they are the naysayers. They like you the way you are, stuck, because many times they are stuck, too. You are allowed to make plans without sharing them with everyone. You may reveal it to them when you are ready or have everything in motion and going your way.

I have different teams, myself, based on the various areas of life. I have those people I call on when I need business advice, personal advice, spiritual advice, etc. Some individuals may be on more than one team. I do not go to my closest girlfriend, who is super at assisting me when I have "female" problems, for a career decision. You get my meaning.

*Empowered by self-confidence,
there is no limit to what you can accomplish.*

6. Cowardice is easy. Don't be afraid to take the plunge. Making a career change may be a scary prospect. Too many people I talk to are afraid to try doing what they love because they are scared they are no good, they will make a mistake, or they're not ready yet. I'm going to let you in on another important component that only the truly successful know and use every day to achieve the success they have. Act in spite of fear.

Show up and be courageous.

That's it. You will always have a healthy fear of the unknown, and you will always make mistakes. If you wait until everything is perfect, you will wait until the day that you are put into your grave. No one is perfect. Most of us are not ever completely prepared to make this kind of commitment. I wasn't.

Relax, let go. Trust you are smart and resourceful enough to course-correct as you go along. Experiment in your quest for greatness, and when you make a mistake, keep going. If it worked for Richard Branson, it can work for you, too!

7. Don't wait around. The longer you wait to make a career change to something you love, the less likely you are to ever do it. This is otherwise known as paralysis by analysis. Act quickly. Fortune favors the bold. Open the business you have been dreaming of, take that trip to Tahiti, go wild in your middle-age crisis. Get started now because, as you get older, you will be less likely to take risks. We only have the now, and everything you need to succeed is available to you.

Do what you believe,
and you will end up where you belong.

8. Take classes. You don't have to know it all. Arm yourself with a cheery disposition, good resources, do your homework, and learn the skills you need to give yourself the best chance at success. Take classes or get professional instruction in the industry that interests you. This is a good way to gauge your talent and endurance.

Exercise the muscle. If you don't, it will atrophy.

9. Don't try to do it all on your own (and why would you want to). While many women may think doing something they love requires they start their own business, this is not always the case. It is possible to be in complete bliss without having to reinvent the wheel. An easier approach may be to find a company that does something related to your hobby or passion and try to get a job there.

For example, a friend of mine loves dogs. Her dream was to start a nonprofit caring for canines. She found a job working for a website that provides pet advice and sells pet medications, which is a great fit for her.

The goal here is to build a passionate life, not to climb Mt. Everest (unless that happens to be your passion). Spend time thinking about what you truly strive for and where you would like to see yourself in five, ten, twenty years.

Our success is measured in how much we love, are loved, give back, and the gem we bring to the planet.

Toni Morrison once spoke about what children really want from their parents. She said, when children enter a room, they want to see their parents' faces beam. To me, that is the greatest measure of my success. If I enter a room, the people in the room are delighted and happy to see me, then I have brightened their day in some way.

I can get more of what I want if I
help other people get more of what they want.

10. Be patient. People pursuing a passion must ready themselves for the early toils that will inevitably occur. If you put yourself on an entrepreneurial avenue, on average, it will take you two years to get to the place where you will start to feel comfortable.

Change takes time.

The Money Will Come ~ No, Trust Me, It Will

Steve Jobs said this in his now oft-repeated commencement address at Stanford. Do what you love. He wasn't concerned about the money. He just kept working at what he loved to do.

You've got to find what you love. That is as accurate for your work as it is for your lovers. Your work is going to fill a large part of your life, and the only way to be truly satisfied is to do what you believe is great work. The only way to do great work is to love what you do. If you haven't found it yet, keep looking. Don't settle. As with all matters of the heart, you'll know when you find it. Like any great relationship, it gets better and better as the years roll on. So, keep looking until you find it. Don't settle.

We are here to make a dent in the Universe.

When you are doing what you love, your whole life seems to kick into gear. You won't even consider what you do to be work. It will feel like play to you. For you to put in long hours or make the sacrifices you need to make to live the life of your dreams is a no-brainer. It will be easy to make those sacrifices. You won't even question them.

Abraham Hicks tells us how to release
resistance to achieve great abundance.
http://www.youtube.com/watch?v=H1rE7vqmbp0

The following is a simple meditation to open up the possibilities:

Choose a place where you feel happy and safe. Take a few minutes to settle down. Notice your breath. Start breathing in deeply and exhaling comfortably. Relaxation is the objective. Don't hold your breath or try to control anything. I find concentrating on my breathing helps. What I mean by that is to notice the rhythm of your breath.

Now that you're relaxed, remove all thoughts from your mind. I have a blank screen in my head at this point of the meditation. You can sit for just 10 minutes in silence with a blank mind. Repeating a mantra is a recommendation to keep thoughts from creeping in. When I seek clarity, I prefer to ask questions. Here are three I like:

Who am I?
Pause for a moment or two, then repeat the question.

What do I want?
Pause for a moment or two, then repeat the question.

How can I serve?
Pause for a moment or two, then repeat the question.

Are you getting any answers? You must be really, really, really quiet to hear the answers.

God is silent until I am.

Worksheets for Chapter Five
Worksheet A: Your Gratitude Journal

It's time for another journal. Every day before you go to sleep, write down everyone and everything you are grateful for. You may repeat the same things from day to day. However, I am going to push you to add more and more items each time you write in your journal. The idea is to be thankful for everything you have in your life. Like I mentioned earlier in this chapter, you asked for everything you currently have. I know you can't believe it, you did!

Worksheet B: Assemble Your Vision Board

Get out a gigantic sheet of paper. You're going to map out your vision for your life. Take Steve's advice. Don't settle. Find the thing that makes your heart sing. Figure out a way to spend the majority of your day doing it and making money at it. Brainstorm. Think outside the box. Throw the box out! Open yourself up to all the countless ways you can make your dream come true. And then, go make it happen!

Follow me as I show how to construct a vision board that will help you to allow a bounty of prosperity, fame, reputation, love, travel, and much more into your life.
www.tarabecker.com

To change it up a bit, using the same layout as the vision board, create your own Achievement Board. Every time you achieve something matching your vision, affix it to your Achievement Board to remind you that you can do it. Watch your vision and passion come to life!

CHAPTER SIX

The Journey Continues from Fear to Freedom

Just because we can't see the big picture,
doesn't mean there isn't one.
~ Elijah Selby

Well, I would say we are at the end of the road, but the truth is, we have only just started! Before I bid you adieu for now, I want to leave you with a few thoughts, small treasures of love and hope you can take with you on your sojourn.

I hope by now you realize how wonderful, remarkable, and lovely you really are. Navigating life is more about understanding the lessons along the way rather than it is about figuring them out. Quit trying so hard. I find, when I let up and go with the flow, I am a magnet for my wishes. I deserve all the best that love and life have to offer.

The rest of my life is the best of my life.

Never stop looking for what's not there. I promise, if you keep searching, you won't be disappointed. Get out of your armchair and into your life. Be fully engaged with the direction of your life. Write it, direct it, and be the star of your story, your movie, your junket. Life is a monumental expedition. Participate! Rejoice!

It's cliché, but there is never a better time than now! Now is all you have, use it the best way you can. Don't let this precious life slip away. Remember, today is a present!

It's time to face your fears. Keep in mind they are illusions; don't let them paralyze you. The choice is yours. You owe it to yourself to be the new you. The best you. It's never too late to begin. If you cooperate in taking care of the Universe, the Universe will take care of you. Just start!

F.E.A.R.
False Evidence Appearing Real

I hope after reading this book, you feel motivated, unstoppable, and invincible, but don't get too cocky. Just when you think you have it all figured out, the Universe will change it up on you. Be prepared for things to get slightly rocky again. Remember, it's all about understanding. Take it easy, ebb and flow with the rhythm of life, it's good for you. Trust you are safe. I will be with you all the way.

True freedom and the end of suffering
is living in such a way as if you had completely chosen
whatever you feel or experience at this moment.
~ Eckhart Tolle

Deepak Chopra reminds us change is a natural part of life. How we react to the change depends on the results we think it will bring. Doubt and uncertainty prevents us from moving forward. It brings about those *what if* questions. *What if I'm not successful? What if it doesn't work out?*

When your present moment continuously generates signals of discomfort, listen to the message, and use it to make positive changes. We can actually look forward to change when we trust the Universe is presenting us with new passages for good. When we are able to understand change in this manner, we can find something positive in it.

> *It may be hard for an egg to turn into a bird:*
> *it would be a jolly sight harder for it to*
> *learn to fly while remaining an egg.*
> *We are like eggs at present.*
> *And you cannot go on indefinitely*
> *being just an ordinary, decent egg.*
> *We must be hatched or go bad.*
> ~ C.S. Lewis

Looking back at our lives, we may see most changes were not only for the best (though we didn't think so at the time), but they allowed us to move into our next evolutionary development. It's time to step out of the ego mind, embrace change, and propel into the uncertainty of the future, knowing it will all work out. Whatever change is imminent, trust it is part of your growth process.

Change may bring us new opportunities to reveal strengths we didn't even know we had. New situations may bring us greater knowledge and problem-solving strategies that allow us to grow and mature. Change may actually surprise us with a new perspective to bring us freedom and accepting change as a natural order of things allows moments of creative genius.

So, we now know life is always changing. If you don't change with it, you'll get stuck. I discovered quite a bit about change by reading the humorous and telling parable, *Who Moved My Cheese?* by Spencer Johnson, M.D. I have always loved this story with cheese as a metaphor. Dr. Johnson details seven steps to keep you on your toes and prepare you to thrive in your life, not just survive. What we are talking about here is that change in life is inevitable. If we are not willing to change with it, life will pass us by. Additionally, by not changing, life will present interesting issues for us to tackle.

> *I want to inspire people to let their true light shine to live a full life and achieve their goals.*
> ~Katy Perry

As my mom always told me, "Life is a journey, not a destination." What I've been addressing here in the book is that living is about the trek and how we respond to the encounters that come up to meet us along the way. My motto, "*The journey is the destination.*"

> *We are living our way into the answers.*

Failure is not the opposite of success but the ways and means to achieve it. The lessons we learn along the path of failure teach us what we need to know to reach success.

Did you know most people stop before they get to the finish line? Successful people will tell you one of the keys to success is perseverance, plain not giving up! As long as you are taking action, you are in the present and out of the ego mind that wants to distract you. Take action now. Just keep moving forward. Don't let a setback stop you.

> *Courage doesn't always roar.*
> *Sometimes courage is the little voice*
> *at the end of the day that says*
> *I'll try again tomorrow.*
> ~ Mary Anne Radmacher

The goal is not to avoid falling. The goal is to get back up, dust yourself off, and start again. There was an interview of a 3-year old girl gymnast. When asked what she does when she falls. The little girl got a puzzled look on her face. She responded, "I get up." You could see the wheels in this little girl's head turning and thinking, "Of course I get up, what else would I do? These crazy grown-ups; they ask the silliest questions."

What's one step you can take today to move toward your dream? Don't hold yourself back. *Do not ask God to guide your footsteps if you are not willing to move your feet.*

Take a chance. What could happen could astonish you. You are in my heart. I cannot wait to see what fun the Universe has in store for all of us. I am still in the middle of my journey and cannot believe how much my life has changed in such a short time. I hope I have given you the courage to go for it and start your own venture. I love you all. I wish you the most loving, happy, and fulfilling lives.

I would love to hear your stories. Please email me to tell me about your travels.

> *Everything will be all right in the end...*
> *if it's not all right, then it's not yet the end.*
> ~ Quote from movie, *Best Exotic Marigold Hotel*

Worksheets for Chapter Six
Worksheet A: Dream Big

The exercises in this chapter come from the great coach, Kym Dolcimascolo
www.kymdolcimascolo.com

Dream. Dream big! I learned this exercise from one of my coaches. She had me be my own screenwriter. She had me write about a day in the life of *me* in the life I wanted to have. Sort of like an act from a movie about you. Write it in present tense. Be as specific as you possibly can. Don't hold back. Be sure to include descriptions of where you are, what you're doing, and what the conversation is like. Go nuts!

Schedule a two-hour appointment with yourself to do this exercise. Don't spend a minute more than two hours.

Now that you have written your act from a day in the life of you, record it. Play this recording before you go to bed each night. Fall asleep listening to it. Then play it again in the morning before you're alert. This is your personal self-hypnosis tape for creating the life you want. Give it a try.

Worksheet B: Characteristics of the New Me

Now that you have your new *day in the life of me* recording, write down the characteristics of the new you. Like I suggested in all of the other chapters, write as many as you can until your hand cramps up. Remember, you aren't doing this once. Add to and refine your list on an ongoing basis. Pick it up once a month and check in with yourself. I am sure there are characteristics on this list you are demonstrating right now and you will continue to display.

Acknowledgements

For my special Circle of Friends...this is for you.

Friends In My Circle

When I was little, I used to believe in the concept of one best
friend,
And then I started to become a woman.
And then I found out that if you allow your heart to open up,
God would show you the best in many friends.
One friend is needed when you're going through things with
your man.
Another friend is needed when you're going through things
with your mom.
Another when you want to shop, share, heal, hurt, joke, or
just be.
One friend will say, *Let's cry together.*
Another, *Let's fight together.*
Another, *Let's walk away together.*
One friend will meet your spiritual need,
Another your shoe fetish,
Another your love for movies,
Another will be with you in your season of confusion,
Another will be your clarifier,
Another the wind beneath your wings.

But whatever their assignment in your life,
On whatever the occasion,
On whatever the day,
Or wherever you need them to meet you with their gym shoes
 on and hair pulled back,
Or to hold you back from making a complete fool of yourself.
Those are your best friends.
It may all be wrapped up in one woman. But for many, it's
 wrapped up in several. One from 7th grade. One from high
 school. Several from college years. A couple from old jobs.
 On some days your mother, On some days your neighbor,
 On others, your sisters,
And on some days, your daughters.
So whether they've been your friend for 20 minutes or 20 years,
 God has placed them in your life to make a difference.

~ Author Unknown

It is with the heartfelt gratitude that I acknowledge the following individuals for their part in my evolution, for it is because of them that I now stand where I am. You have been with me, many by my side, while I have learned, loved, felt hurt, been angry, expressed compassion, grown spiritually, suffered gut-wrenching agony, moved forward and backward and forward again, and most of all, have lived and lived and lived. And you have afforded me the space and the comfort to share the limitless emotions that this path has offered me. Thank you for being there for me and for your continued contributions to my progression. Words alone cannot express how much I appreciate everything you have done for me...my friends, my teachers, my confidants.

I would first like to acknowledge my late husband, Rick Becker, who was then and is now my soul mate. Rick, if it was not for you, I would not be embarking upon this voyage. I feel you and thank you for your undying support and encouragement, even from beyond. I "get it" now!

I would especially like to thank my two sons, Dillon and Ryan, who have made me so proud to be their Mom. You mean the world to me.

Thank you to my Mom and Dad. I'm so grateful for the good things that I got from each of you. I hope you see them in me.

To my exceptional friends, both past and present, who have cheered me on, championed me, been my mirror, and who, regardless of whether they know it, have always been with me on this jaunt. First, I thank Bo Freeman (and family), who through her support this book could be published. For their support, shout outs to Alex Bruzzese, Jennifer Seeley, and Heather Wainer. For helping me keep my sense of humor, I thank Laurie and Jim Taylor and Morgan Stadick. For being such great examples, I thank Cheryl Burget, Dr. Anastasia Alexander, Jade Rehder, Joanna Kennedy, and Gayle Goodrich.

To my soul sisters, who have left an indelible mark on my heart and on my spirit, you have been and will remain my friends, my relentless defenders, my advocates, and my teachers. I love you and am indebted to you and to the sweet sound of your names. Thank you Jenny Rush, Kristina Darling, Karen Rudat, Lynzi Cohen, Lorraine Brown, and Marsha van Dongeren.

I would like to acknowledge and thank my guardians and role models from whom I have learned so much and who continue to teach me. Thank you Aaron Anderson, Barbara Daoust,

Miwa Linehan, Mee Vaj, Tracey Fitzgerald, Kym Dolcimascolo, Sue Frederick, Zoilita Grant, and Janene Brunk.

Thank you to Jana Stanfield and Jen Hannah for bringing their inspirational music into my life and for always lifting my spirits. I'm so grateful that I had your music with me.

I am beholden to you R.F. You taught me a lot of lessons about myself. Without you, I would not have gotten through one of the hardest years of my life.

I would also like to thank my delightful golden retriever, Cinnamon, whose unconditional love always kept me going, and some days was my only reason to get out of bed.

I would like to recognize the following individuals, a few of whom I've actually had the pleasure of meeting, who have inspired me and have imparted great wisdom to me that fosters me still. Thank you Doreen Virtue, Janet Bray Attwood and Chris Attwood, Mark Victor Hanson, Mark Yuzuik, Jack Canfield, Brandon Bays, Byron Katie, Dr. Wayne Dyer, Michael Beckwith, and Dr. and Master Zhi Gang Sha.

There are so many more people who have made an impact on my life. You know who you are, and I want you to know that your positive influence on my life has been important to me. My gratitude to you is boundless.

Bibliography/Resources

Abraham, Esther Hicks, and Jerry Hicks. *The Law of Attraction: The Basics of the Teachings of Abraham*. Carlsbad, CA: Hay House, 2006. Print.

Aramburo, Carolina. *Professional Business Coaching*. N.p., n.d. Web. 10 Aug. 2013. <http://carolinaaramburo.com/>.

Armstrong, Alison A. *The Queen's Code*. The Queen's Code, n.d. Web. 10 Aug. 2013. <http://www.queenscode.com/>.

Attwood, Janet Bray and Chris Attwood. *The Passion Test: The Effortless Path to Discovering Your Life Purpose*. New York: Penguin, 2008. Print.

Bays, Brandon. *Freedom Is*. London: Hodder Mobius, 2006. Print.

Benton, Jim. *It's Happy Bunny: Life, Get One: And Other Words of Wisdom and Junk That Will Make You Wise or Something*. New York: Scholastic, 2005. Print.

Bernstein, Gabrielle.

Case, Ted. *Inspirational Gravity*. Wilsonville: Case Dynamics, 2007. Print.

Chapman, Gary D. *The Five Love Languages: How to Express Heartfelt Commitment to Your Mate*. Chicago: Northfield Publishers, 1995. Print.

Creager, Todd. *The Long, Hot Marriage*. Sevierville: Insight, 2008. Print.

Daoust, Barbara. *True Love True Self*. N.p.: Enchanted Forest, 2012. Print.

Dyer, Wayne W. *Change Your Thoughts, Change Your Life: Living the Wisdom of the Tao*. Carlsbad, CA: Hay House, 2007. Print.

Dyer, Wayne W. *Inspiration: Your Ultimate Calling*. Carlsbad, CA: Hay House, 2006. Print.

Dyer, Wayne W. *Wishes Fulfilled: Mastering the Art of Manifesting*. Carlsbad, CA: Hay House, 2012. Print.

Forleo, Marie. *Make Every Man Want You: How to Be so Irresistible You'll Barely Keep from Dating Yourself!* New York: McGraw-Hill, 2008. Print.

Frederick, Sue. *Bridges to Heaven: True Stories of Loved Ones on the Other Side*. New York: St. Martin's, 2013. Print.

Frederick, Sue. *I See Your Dream Job: A Career Intuitive Shows You How to Discover What You Were Put on Earth to Do*. New York: St. Martin's, 2009. Print.

Frederick, Sue. *I See Your Soul Mate*. New York: St. Martin's, 2012. Print.

Freedman, Rory, and Kim Barnouin. *Skinny Bitch*. [S.l.]: Running, 2005. Print.

Geisel, Theodor Seuss. *Seuss-isms: Wise and Witty Prescriptions for Living from the Good Doctor.* New York: Random House, 1997. Print.

Gikandi, David Cameron. *A Happy Pocket Full of Money: Infinite Wealth and Abundance in the Here and Now.* Charlottesville, VA: Hampton Roads, 2011. Print.

Grant, Zoilita, MS, and Neal Rohr. *The Self Healing Book.* N.p.: Master Key Incorporated, 1997. Print.

Johnson, Spencer. *Who Moved My Cheese?: An A-mazing Way to Deal with Change in Your Work and in Your Life.* New York: Putnam, 1998. Print.

Katie, Byron, and Stephen Mitchell. *Loving What Is: Four Questions That Can Change Your Life.* New York: Harmony, 2002. Print.

Millman, Dan. *The Life You Were Born to Live: A Guide to Finding Your Life Purpose.* Tiburon, CA: HJ Kramer, 1993. Print.

Morris, Cindy. *Priestess Entrepreneur: Keep Your Soul Surviving as Your Business Is Thriving.* Garden City, NY: Morgan James Publishing, 2008. Print.

Smith, Marilyn. *Gratitude: A Key to Happiness.* N.p.: n.p., n.d. *Dr. and Master Zhi Gang Sha.* Web. <http://storefront.drsha.com/gratitude-a-key-to-happiness-by-marilyn-smith.html>.

Tolle, Eckhart. *A New Earth: Awakening to Your Life's Purpose.* New York: Plume, 2006. Print.

Printed in the United States
By Bookmasters